MY PET
TURTLE

Lynn Hamilton

Weigl Publishers Inc.

Published by Weigl Publishers Inc.
350 5th Avenue, Suite 3304 PMB 6G
New York, NY 10118-0069
Website: www.weigl.com

Project Coordinator
Heather C. Hudak

Design
Terry Paulhus

Library of Congress Cataloging-in-Publication Data available upon request.
Fax 1-866-44-WEIGL for the attention of the Publishing Records department.

ISBN 978-1-60596-088-3 (hard cover)
ISBN 978-1-60596-089-0 (soft cover)

Printed in the United States of America
1 2 3 4 5 6 7 8 9 0   13 12 11 10 09

Photograph and Text Credits

Every reasonable effort has been made to trace ownership and to obtain permission to reprint copyright
material. The publishers would be pleased to have any errors or omissions brought to their attention so that
they may be corrected in subsequent printings.

Weigl acknowledges Getty Images as its primary image supplier for this title.

Contents

A Turtle World

Turtles provide a fascinating link to the past. Turtles living today have many of the same traits as turtles from millions of years ago. People have been fascinated by these unique creatures for centuries.

Choosing a turtle for a pet is a long-term commitment. Healthy pet turtles can live for more than 20 years.

Turtles are most recognized for the sturdy and beautiful shells that they carry on their backs. Keeping a turtle as a pet allows you to bring a part of nature into your life.

Turtles do not chirp or purr, and they are not cuddly pets. They do not race to meet you at the door. In fact, they usually move very slowly on land. Do not be fooled by the quiet nature of turtles. All turtles have different personalities and routines. Turtles can be very active and can be great fun to observe.

Caring for a pet turtle is challenging. Owners must recreate the turtle's natural environment. A turtle owner must become familiar with turtle behavior. Someone who understands turtles will know that a turtle will hide in his shell when he is alarmed. Learning about turtles and their needs is an important part of making a healthy home for a pet turtle.

Turtle Types

- There are about 250 types of turtles.
- There are many different names for turtles. Land turtles are called tortoises. Turtles that live in fresh water are called aquatic, or water, turtles. Ocean turtles are called sea turtles.
- Nearly two million homes in the U.S. have at least one pet turtle.
- Water turtles have lighter shells than land turtles. Webs between their toes act as flippers to propel the turtles through the water.
- African pancake tortoises live in rocky places. They have soft, flat shells that allow them to hide between the rocks.

Pet Profiles

Many factors will influence the type of turtle you choose as a pet. Some turtles are mostly land animals. Others spend much of their time in the water. Most turtles spend time on land and in the water. If the climate is suitable, many turtles can be kept outdoors. Some turtles **hibernate** and will need a special place to do so safely. While turtles do not need to be walked, brushed, or cuddled, they are still a big responsibility. Turtles require special care to live a long, healthy life. They need to live in a tank called an aquarium. They need to be fed and groomed regularly. Turtles must also visit a **veterinarian** at least once a year.

RED-EARED SLIDER

- Grows about 11 or 12 inches (28 or 30 centimeters) in length
- Olive-green skin with yellow markings; has red patches near the ears
- Likes to swim, but needs dry land, too
- Active during the day
- May be aggressive toward other turtles or people
- Can live more than 25 years

SPOTTED TURTLE

- Grows about 5 inches (13 cm) in length
- **Carapace** is black with yellow spots
- Males' eyes are brown; females' eyes are yellow
- Mostly **carnivorous**
- Likes to swim
- May be aggressive toward other turtles

MUSK TURTLE

- Grows about 4 to 6 inches (10 to 15 cm) in length
- Sprays a smelly liquid when upset
- Climbs well
- Mostly carnivorous
- May be aggressive toward other turtles
- Closely related to the mud turtle

BOX TURTLE

- Grows 6 to 8 inches (15 to 20 cm) in length
- Lives between 30 and 40 years
- Brown or black carapace with yellow, orange, and brown markings
- Able to tuck their arms and legs inside their hinged shell
- Eats both plants and meat

PAINTED TURTLE

- Grows about 8 to 10 inches (20 to 25 cm) in length
- Lives to be about 20 years old
- Some red markings on carapace and legs; yellow markings on the head
- Needs an aquarium with a **basking** surface
- Active during the day

WOOD TURTLE

- Grows to about 10 inches (25 cm) in length
- Lives to be at least 25 years old
- **Scutes** are in the shape of four-sided peaks
- Needs both water and land areas
- Enjoys digging and climbing
- May learn to recognize their owner

Turtles through Time

About 200 million years ago, turtles shared the land with dinosaurs. The oldest turtle **fossils** were found in Germany. These fossils show that early turtles had heavy shells. Unlike present-day turtles, ancient turtles had teeth. They could not pull their necks into their shells. Their necks and tails were covered in a spiny armor, or protective covering.

Before buying a turtle, contact game or wildlife authorities about state laws. Make sure your choice is legal.

Turtles **adapted** to their different environments. For example, sea turtles have paddle-like legs and flat shells that make them good swimmers. Land turtles have thick, strong shells that protect them from **predators**.

People have had relationships with turtles for centuries. Turtles appear in the creation stories told by Native Americans and Asian peoples. Live turtles were sometimes loaded onto ships to be used as food during long ocean voyages. Turtle shells have been used to make items such as jewelry. Turtles have also been collected from nature and sold as pets.

For these reasons, some turtle populations are dangerously low. In the United States and many other countries, **endangered** turtles are now protected by law. People have also formed special organizations to raise awareness and to help turtle populations survive.

Reptile Relatives

- Turtles are reptiles. Reptiles are cold-blooded animals that have scales and lungs. They lay eggs on land. Other reptiles are alligators, crocodiles, lizards, and snakes.

- Giant tortoises live on the Galapagos Islands, west of South America. They can weigh more than 500 pounds (227 kilograms) and can live for more than 100 years.
- Turtles live on every continent except Antarctica.

Life Cycle

Some turtles are collected from nature. Other turtles are born and raised in captivity. Special laws are in place to protect turtle populations. Turtles have specific needs at different times in their lives. Knowing the many stages of your turtle's life will help you care for your pet.

Eggs

All mother turtles, whether land or water turtles, lay their eggs on land. The mother digs a hole, usually in a sunny area, and lays the eggs inside. She covers the eggs with soil and plant matter to keep them safe and warm. There may be a few eggs or hundreds of eggs. The eggs are left in the hole for at least 2 to 3 months, depending on the kind of turtle. To protect eggs from predators and cold weather, turtle breeders sometimes move the eggs to an **incubator**.

Hatchlings

It can take minutes, hours, or even a few days for a baby turtle to hatch from its egg. Turtles break out from the egg using an egg tooth. An egg tooth is a sharp point on the tip of a turtle's beak-like jaw. The egg tooth falls off after the turtle has hatched. Hatchlings must dig up through their protective coverings to reach the surface.

Baby Turtles

Baby turtles should be kept in a separate enclosure, away from adult turtles. Baby turtles will not eat for about one week. Instead, they feed off the yolk sac that is attached to their **plastron**. Once it is no longer needed, the yolk sac detaches from their body. Baby turtles require special nutrition for their shells to develop properly.

Growth and Maturity

By age three, turtles have reached about one-third of their adult size. This is about four times their size at birth. By six years of age, turtles are two-thirds grown. As turtles age, their growth slows. Turtles live to different ages. The length of a turtle's life depends on its species, the environment, and the quality of care it receives.

living life

- Growth rings on a turtle's shell tell a little about the growing stages of a turtle, but they are not a way to tell the age of a turtle.
- Turtle eggs and hatchlings are easy targets for predators. In nature, only a few turtles out of hundreds may survive to reach maturity.

Picking Your Pet

Choosing a pet turtle requires careful thought. Be sure the choice you are making is the best one for you and your pet. Think about the following questions as you make this important decision.

Turtles carry **salmonella**, which can make young children ill. Children under age eight should not keep pet turtles.

Can I Provide a Good Home for a Turtle?

Whether in an indoor tank or an outdoor enclosure, turtles need a clean home with plenty of space for their activities. Aquariums can be heavy and should rest on a sturdy surface. The temperature must be carefully controlled. Turtles require protection from animals such as birds, cats, dogs, rodents, and snakes. Owners should always provide a secure space that is away from danger and disturbances.

What Will a Turtle Cost?

Although some turtles are inexpensive, setting up an aquarium or outdoor space can be costly. Cleaning products, tank supplies, and food are regular expenses. Turtles should also be taken to the veterinarian once a year. If your turtle is sick, you may have to buy medication.

Am I Ready to Care for a Turtle?

Adopting a pet turtle means learning about your turtle's needs and following daily routines. You should set aside time each day to spend with your turtle. If you are away from home, you will need to ask a reliable person to care for your pet.

Mother Nature

- It is unsafe to release a pet turtle into nature. The local environment may not match the turtle's natural environment. The turtle may not be able to survive the outdoor climate and could die.

Tanks for Turtles

Aquariums usually make a good home for a turtle. A sturdy plastic container may also work. Cover the bottom of the tank with materials such as artificial grass or gravel from a pet store. Be careful which materials you use inside your turtle's aquarium. Some are hard to clean. Others may have small particles that your turtle might swallow. When planning his house, remember that some turtles need a place to dig and burrow.

Some plants are poisonous to turtles. Before putting plants inside your turtle's tank, make sure they are not a danger.

14

Pet turtles require a water container for wading or swimming. Water turtles need more swimming room. Most turtles need a dry surface for basking. Your turtle will need a ramp to climb out of the water. You will also require a special heater to warm the water and a system that filters the water to keep it clean. Thermometers tell the temperature of the air and water inside the aquarium. A proper cover over the enclosure will keep your turtle safe from small children and other pets.

Turtles need sunlight or lighting with ultraviolet B (UVB) rays to stay healthy. The lighting should match the natural changes in sunlight. A heating light should also be placed above one end of the basking area.

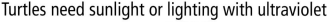

Hide and Seek

- Turtles like to have a place to hide. Such places could be a cave made of flat stones, a hollowed log, or a wooden box.

- Some turtles can be kept outside during the warm, summer months. You will need an enclosure that can be covered with wire mesh to protect your turtle from outdoor predators.

Turtle Treats

Turtles need a varied diet to stay healthy, but they are fussy about their food. To make sure your turtle eats a healthy mix of food, chop his meal into very small pieces. This way, your turtle will not be able to pick out his favorite foods. Fruit, vegetables, and other plant foods are an important part of a healthy diet. Examples include blueberries, cantaloupe, carrots, cauliflower, cucumbers, dandelion greens, peas, and tomatoes.

Spinach causes kidney problems in turtles. Rhubarb leaves are poisonous to turtles.

Some turtles prefer a diet with more meat. This could include crayfish, earthworms, freshwater shrimp, insects, snails, and trout. Worms and turtle food are available at pet stores.

Young turtles should be fed daily. Older turtles can be fed less often. Some turtles only need to be fed two to five days per week. Other turtles like to be fed small amounts of food two or three times each day. A turtle may overeat. Bulging legs, underside, and tail are signs of an overweight turtle.

Water turtles generally eat in the water, and land turtles eat on land. Turtles of different sizes should be separated during feeding so that they do not bite each other when reaching for food. A veterinarian can suggest the best food and a feeding schedule for your type of turtle.

Healthy Habits

- Turtles need calcium to keep their shells and bones healthy. Calcium, vitamin, and mineral **supplements** are available at pet stores.
- Be sure that food picked or caught outside has not been exposed to chemicals such as weed killers. Chemicals can be poisonous to your turtle. It is important to wash fruits, vegetables, and other plant foods before feeding them to your pet.

- Your turtle may wade in the water from which she drinks. This water must be changed at least once a day.

Shells and Such

Turtles' physical features are well suited to their way of life. Understanding your turtle's physical traits will help you create a home that matches your pet's natural environment and needs.

8 Essential Parts of the Turtle

Unlike humans, turtles do not have ears. Instead, their eardrums are found under the skin or scales, just behind their cheeks. Turtles are able to hear low, deep sounds. Vibrations are also passed through the legs or shell to the ear.

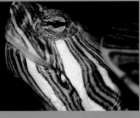

Land turtles have strong legs to support their heavy shells. Water turtles have long claws and webbed feet. Land turtles have shorter, separate toes that are better suited to land activities such as digging.

Turtles have a keen sense of smell. This enables them to locate and select their food. A turtle may or may not like certain foods, depending on the smell. Water turtles can smell underwater.

The carapace is joined to the plastron by bony bridges. The surface of the shell is made of **keratin**. Different sections on the shell are called scutes. A turtle cannot detach from his shell.

A turtle's skin is covered with scales. Scales help prevent moisture loss.

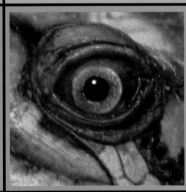

Turtles can spot food and dangerous predators from a distance because they have excellent eyesight.

Turtles do not have teeth. Instead, they use the sharp edges of their strong jaws to crush their food.

Most turtles have short tails. Male turtles have longer, thicker, and more pointed tails than female turtles. This is one way to tell males apart from females.

Turtle Polish

A clean home is essential for a healthy turtle. Some turtle owners feed their turtles in a small, separate tank or container to help keep the main tank clean. Waste and uneaten food should be removed often. Water containers should be washed daily, too.

Painting a turtle's shell can be dangerous to his health and should never be done.

Every two to four weeks, move your turtle to a temporary container so that you can clean his tank. Aquarium glass, rocks, and other surfaces should be cleaned with a safe cleanser and rinsed well. Lining materials should be washed or replaced.

The water in an aquarium should be changed every two or three days. You will not need to change the water as often if you place a filter in the tank. The filter should be checked regularly and cleaned when needed.

Like human fingernails, turtles' claws do not stop growing. A turtle's beak is always growing, too. Daily activities wear down a turtle's claws and jaw, but sometimes not enough. Long claws can keep a turtle from walking properly. An overgrown beak can make chewing difficult. A veterinarian can trim your turtle's claws and beak if necessary.

Turtle Ticks

- Turtles that spend time outside in the summer may get small **parasites** called ticks in the folds of their skin. Dabbing a tick with some rubbing alcohol will loosen its hold. Use a tick puller or tweezers to remove the pest.

Healthy and Happy

When you choose your turtle, make sure to select a healthy one. A healthy turtle will have clear eyes. Its shell should be firm and have few cracks. The turtle should be able to breathe easily with a closed mouth. Healthy water turtles are able to swim easily below the surface. A turtle should feel solid, not light. Check the folds of skin on the arms and legs for parasites.

Do not allow your turtle to wander on grass that has been treated with chemicals. Chemicals can make your turtle sick.

If you are adding another turtle to your tank, a period of **quarantine** for the new turtle should prevent the spread of disease. A minimum of four weeks should ensure your new turtle is not sick. Providing your turtle with a clean

home and well-balanced diet will help keep her well. A good appetite is another sign of a healthy turtle.

As you become more familiar with your turtle, you will learn which behaviors and appearances are normal. Watch for changes. Has her appetite changed? Does she have swollen or runny eyes? Swelling, unusual breathing sounds, sores, or a softening shell are signs of illness. These conditions may require a visit to a veterinarian. As long as your turtle is healthy, a yearly checkup should be suitable.

Sometimes, a trip to the veterinarian is not needed to fix a simple problem. For example, if your turtle flips over onto her shell, she may not be able to right herself. You can gently help her turn over.

Shell Shockers

- Some turtles do not swim well and can drown in water that is deeper than the top of their shell. If the water level is too low, a flipped turtle may not be able to right himself and could drown.
- Dropping your turtle can crack her shell. **Fungus** can grow in a crack or injury on your turtle's shell. It will appear as a cottony white film on the surface of your turtle.
- Turtles rely on their environment to stay warm. They are sensitive to changes in temperature. Because of this, always add lukewarm water to the tank. Placing the aquarium away from doors and open windows prevents drafts.

Turtle Behavior

Turtles do not need to share their home with other turtles to be content. Sometimes, turtles do not get along with other turtles. Before adding more turtles to the tank, find out if your turtle is aggressive or if he enjoys having company. The more turtles you have, the larger the tank should be.

Tapping on the glass of the tank, vibrations from a loud noise, or pounding footsteps may disturb your turtle and cause stress. Stressed turtles may become sick.

Most turtles do not enjoy being handled. They might tuck into their shells, kick, or try to bite when lifted. Usually, it is best to lift or hold your turtle only when necessary, such as cleaning times or health checks. Small turtles can be held in the palm of your hand. Turtles like the security of a surface under their feet. Guard small turtles with your hand to keep them from falling.

A large turtle can be lifted by placing one hand on each side of his body. Place your thumbs on the carapace and your fingers under the plastron. Land turtles are more likely to enjoy having their head or shell stroked.

In the right environment, your turtle will want to be more active. You can make your turtle's home interesting. Stones and tree branches make good hiding and climbing spots.

Pet Peeves

Turtles do not like:
- tapping on the tank's glass
- loud noises
- dirty water
- too much attention
- car rides
- having their shells painted

Turtle Talk

- If you feed your turtle in the same area of the tank at the same time each day, he may learn to meet you when you arrive with dinner.
- When taking a small turtle to the veterinarian, you can carry him in a light cotton bag such as a pillow case. To keep your turtle secure and to prevent too much movement, place the bag in a box and tie the top. Make sure your turtle stays upright. Be very careful that your turtle stays warm.

Troubles and Triumphs

Some people are interested in protecting the well-being of turtles. In nature, turtle populations have been dropping at an alarming rate. Turtles have survived for millions of years, but they are now in danger because of human activities. Turtles have been removed from nature to be used for food, to make products, and to become pets. Pollution and other changes to the turtles' natural environment have reduced their numbers, too. Action is being taken to ensure the survival of these wonderful animals. Many countries have passed laws to protect endangered turtles.

Turtle Tales

"The Tortoise and the Hare" is one of *Aesop's Fables*. It is about a hare who brags of his speed. The hare thinks it is funny when the tortoise suggests that they race. When the race begins, the hare speeds past the tortoise. The tortoise follows slowly and steadily. Certain he will win the race, the hare decides he has time to take a nap. The tortoise passes the hare. When the hare wakes up, it is too late. The tortoise has already crossed the finish line. The moral of the story is that slow and steady wins the race.

Taken from *Aesop's Fables*.

Over the years, turtles have appeared in many books and movies. In 1950, the famous children's author Dr. Seuss wrote about turtles in his book *Yertle the Turtle*. In this book, King Yertle orders his kingdom to build him a throne from their shells. Hundreds of turtles pile on top of each other, with Yertle at the top. The throne breaks when one small turtle at the bottom of the pile decides he no longer wants to be a part of the throne.

Since the late 1980s, cartoon characters called the Teenage Mutant Ninja Turtles have starred in many comics, television shows, and movies. These four turtles gained superhero powers when a chemical spilled on them. Now, Donatello, Leonardo, Michelangelo, and Raphael spend their days fighting villains in New York City.

Turtle Trade

- In 1975, it became illegal to sell turtles smaller than 4 inches (10 cm) in length. A small turtle could fit inside a child's mouth and pass on salmonella. This law was intended to prevent small children from getting this bacteria.

- The Convention on International Trade in Endangered Species (CITES) has been signed by 160 countries. Endangered animals on a CITES list have special protection. It is illegal to take those animals into or out of the United States.

Pet Puzzlers

How much do you know about turtles? If you can answer the following questions correctly, you may be ready to own a pet turtle.

Q Will my turtle mix well with other animals?

A Other animals, such as birds, cats, dogs, rodents, and snakes, may eat turtles. Turtles carry salmonella, which may put other pets at risk. Some turtles may not get along with other turtles.

Q What items are poisonous to a turtle?

A Some plants are toxic to turtles. Turtles should also be kept away from foods, soils, or outdoor areas and plants that have been treated with chemicals.

Q Can my turtle go outside of the house?

A If the climate is right, some turtles can live outside in a secure enclosure. During backyard visits, turtles must be protected from predators and poisonous materials. For a short trip to the veterinarian, carry your turtle upright in a light cotton bag. Make sure he stays warm.

Q What feeding routines will my turtle need?

A Young turtles should be fed daily. Older turtles need to eat between two and five times each week. Your veterinarian can advise you about foods, quantities, and schedules for your type of turtle.

Q What does the law say about owning a turtle?

A Laws restrict which turtles can legally be taken from nature, raised, and sold. Endangered turtles on the CITES list cannot be taken into or out of the United States. Turtles smaller than 4 inches (10 cm) may not be sold.

Q Do turtles have a sense of smell?

A Turtles have a very good sense of smell. They use their sense of smell to locate food. Water turtles can smell underwater.

Q How do I keep my turtle happy and healthy?

A Provide a home that is like the turtle's home in nature. Keep the home clean and the temperature constant. Offer a balanced diet. Make sure that your turtle receives the right amount of UVB rays. Take your pet for yearly checkups, and watch for unusual behaviors and changes in appearance.

Turtle Tags

Before you buy your pet turtle, write down some turtle names you like. Some names may work better for a female turtle. Others may suit a male turtle. Here are just a few suggestions.

Scooter
Speedy
Tommy
Sunny
Myrtle
Peanut
Peek-a-Boo
Shelly
Homer
Tucker

Frequently Asked Questions

Does my turtle need to hibernate?

Some turtles, such as box turtles, hibernate when the temperature drops in autumn and winter. They dig themselves under a layer of earth and sleep for several weeks. Turtles that would normally hibernate in nature may not do so as pets. A decreased appetite may be a sign that your turtle wants to hibernate.

Who is at risk for salmonella?

Some people should never come in contact with any reptile. Such people include elderly or sick people, babies, and children under 8 years old, pregnant women, people on antibiotics, and people with immune system disorders. Anyone is at risk if proper precautions are not taken.

What can a turtle owner do to prevent salmonella poisoning?

To prevent salmonella poisoning, always wash your hands thoroughly with disinfectant soap after handling your pet, the tank, or its accessories. Do not let your turtle wander throughout the kitchen or other places where food is kept, prepared, or eaten. You should not use the kitchen sink to clean the tank or accessories.

TURTLE XING

More Information

Animal Organizations

You can help turtles stay healthy and happy by learning more about them. Many organizations are dedicated to teaching people how to care for and protect their pet pals. For more turtle information, write to the following organizations.

The Chicago Turtle Club
6125 N. Fairfield Avenue
Chicago, IL 60659

San Diego Turtle & Tortoise Society
P.O. Box 712514
Santee, CA 92072

Websites

To answer more of your turtle questions, go online and surf to the following websites.

The Reptiles: Turtles and Tortoises
www.pbs.org/wnet/nature/reptiles/turtles_pets.html

My Pets
www.mypets.net.au/flex/turtles/192/1

California Turtle & Tortoise Club
www.tortoise.org

Words to Know

adapted: became used to something

basking: laying under a heat source to warm oneself

carapace: the part of a turtle's shell that is on the back

carnivorous: meat-eating

endangered: animals whose populations are so low that they are in danger of disappearing completely

fossils: remains of ancient animals and plants from long ago found in rocks

fungus: a plant-like organism that appears as fuzz on the skin

hibernate: to spend a period of time in a sleep-like state

incubator: a container used to keep eggs warm so that they will hatch

keratin: the strong substance that makes a turtle's shell hard; the same substance found in human fingernails

parasites: organisms that live on or in other living beings

plastron: the section of a turtle's shell that is under the belly

predators: animals that hunt and kill other animals for food

quarantine: temporary separation from others

salmonella: a type of bacteria that causes flu-like symptoms that can lead to death

scutes: bony plates on a turtle's shell

supplements: things that are added to something to make it better

veterinarian: animal doctor

Index